THE PATH TO SUCCESS IS YOURS

A Journey from Adversity to Empowerment

Wrenn Johnson Ph.D

Written by Wrenn Johnson, Ph.D

978-1-917728-00-3
Copyright © Wrenn Johnson 2025
All intellectual property rights including copyright, design right and publishing rights rest with the author. No part of this book may be copied, reproduced, or transmitted in any way without written permission of the author. Published in Ireland by Orla Kelly Publishing.

Orla Kelly Publishing,
27 Kilbrody,
Mount Oval,
Rochestown,
Cork.
Ireland

Who This Book is For

Are self-doubt, limited resources, or life's challenges holding you back? Wrenn Johnson, a retired Chief of Police turned performance expert, shares her powerful journey from humble beginnings to leadership, proving that success is possible for anyone.

In this inspiring and actionable guide, Wrenn provides practical strategies to overcome adversity, break free from traditional work models, and build your own path to success. Whether you're dreaming of personal growth or entrepreneurial ventures, this book will empower you to embrace resilience, pursue your goals with confidence, and redefine what's possible.

It's time to take that first step—your journey starts here.

Dedication

I want to dedicate this book to everyone who doubted that they were smart enough, had enough money, support, or time to realize their dream. You ARE smart enough. Never give money the power to stop you from doing anything you want to do. Support is nice, but not necessary. Time goes on with or without you, so take advantage of this very minute and do something you want to do, that you need to do. Remember, no person succeeds alone. Every person you meet on the path to your success contributes in some way to that success. So, celebrate those that encourage and help you along the way and appreciate those that stand in your way and force you to go around them or through them to get to where you want to be.

I would like to thank all those who supported, helped, encouraged, or challenged me to begin and complete this project. I owe a great debt to the friends and co-workers who supported and encouraged me to complete it, especially those who seemed to struggle and rejoice with me through each part of the process. My family has always been supportive, even on days when they did not understand what I was doing or why I needed to do it. To those who challenged me prior to, during, and in the future to reach the top of every mountain, words cannot express the gratitude I have for you. Not every person who challenged me was my friend, but each one of them contributed to my success.

Whether it's the earth, the water, or the sky that motivates you, look for it.

Table Of Contents

Who This Book Is For iii

Dedication iv

Chapter One: You And The Author 1

Chapter Two: Success Comes To Those…. 8

Chapter Three: What If? 11

Chapter Four: So, How Do I Plan To Succeed? 18

Chapter Five: Be Inspired 27

Chapter Six: Motivation 32

Chapter Seven: What If I Fail? 45

Chapter Eight: Attacking The Hill… Aka Your Fears 52

Final Thoughts 59

About Wrenn 61

Work with Wrenn 62

Please Review 63

CHAPTER ONE
You And The Author

I am E. Wrenn Johnson (the E. stands for Elizabeth, a name that never seemed to fit me or my personality) and I was born and raised in Guilford County, North Carolina. I was educated in public schools and told from a very early age that I would attend college and become a teacher. What they (my parents, teachers, counsellors) never told me was "how" I was going to get there and, most importantly, how I would pay for it. My mother was a teenager when I was born but was (and still is) one of the smartest women that I know. My father was (and still is) one of the most involved and hardest-working parents that I've ever seen. Together, they were a force to be reckoned with when it came to raising two children who both began their respective paths to success from very different vantage points and with very different paths to follow.

I attended UNC-Wilmington, and quit with one semester to go before graduating with a degree in Physical Education because I didn't want to teach. The thought of teaching was terrifying to me and I thought there just had to be a job out there somewhere that wasn't as scary. I drifted a few years until finally, my mother took me to the High Point Police Department to introduce me to the recruiter for their department. To make a long story short (which is a favorite quote from one of my best friends), that's how I began a very challenging and satisfying career in law enforcement.

I finished basic law enforcement training (BLET) and went to work at the Morehead City Police Department when I was 25 years old. Several things worked to my advantage immediately at the police department. I looked younger than 25, I was fearless (or crazy - I'm not sure which), and I immediately fell in love with the job of being a police officer and wanted to make it a career. I had no idea what challenges and/or brick walls would present themselves in the course of that 29-year career, but I knew immediately that I wanted to experience every bit of it.

During that time, I worked for three Police Chiefs, all of whom had very different ideas of what a police department (PD) was supposed to look like and how officers and employees were to perform. I finished my bachelor's degree, my master's degree, several prestigious management schools, and almost finished my Ph.D. prior to leaving the department. My most important accomplishment at the PD? I think there were many, but none more important than empowering and encouraging several women (and men) who came after me to reach for their dreams and refuse to be stopped before they got there. I am also very proud of the diversity that came to the police department and the success of many programs began while I was there. I am extremely proud to have been a part of that profession and hopefully to have contributed in some small way to helping better either someone's life or bettering a profession whose only mission is to protect the citizens of this country, one jurisdiction at a time.

The most important thing to know about me is that I'm not much different from you. I was born to very young parents who struggled, like many of you, to pay the bills each month and put food on the table. Neither of my parents were well educated, but both "did the best they could do" each day to raise my sister and me. We were raised in a very conservative, religious household and were very restricted in what we saw, what we did, and how we were allowed to act both in public and in private. I was very blessed to be a part of a very loving and supportive family, one that differed from me in so many ways that I often struggled to be a part of them rather than apart from them.

My story is about refusing to quit and, more importantly, refusing to fail. It is not about someone who has had an easy life or who has never had to work. I have had a very happy life and have been very fortunate, but it has certainly not always been easy, nor has it been one without bad days and, sometimes, bad weeks. I have always found a way to improve things, primarily because I never panicked or ran away from trouble or day-to-day problems. I believe that every problem has a solution and that somehow, I will always be able to find that solution. Being poor was always just a situation; it was never "who I was," so it never stopped me from doing what I wanted to do.

As you continue to read this book and hopefully become inspired in some way to change something in your life, you will note that my life is not much different from yours. Honestly, you could have written this book but for some reason you chose not to. I am asking you to change something in your life that makes it better, and it really doesn't matter what that is. It might be that you want to be a better parent and be more involved in your children's lives. If that's the case, then be better organized and participate more, but don't stop because life is complicated or you feel you don't have time. When your children have left home, all you will have is time and you better hope that you enjoyed them while they were young. My son married his childhood sweetheart and they now have children of their own. I am so glad I got to enjoy all those years with him when he was young. So, what have you learned about the author of this book? I hope you have learned that I am well educated, but not because I had wealthy parents who let me attend school and party until I graduated with a degree from college. I am well educated because I invested the time and money in myself (sometimes at great personal expense where I borrowed but always paid it back). I hope that you learned that I was raised by very loving parents that supported me, sometimes when I was not necessarily the person that they had hoped that I would be. They did the very best they could with what they knew and what they had to raise us, and I turned out ok. Most importantly, that I recognize their strengths and built on them in my own life and that at no point in my life have I ever blamed them for my own shortcomings or struggles.

I also hope that you learned that each day is a new day and that you can be something different today than you were yesterday. I was raised to be a teacher, and even though I never taught in public or private schools, I never considered myself a failure because of it. I was raised in a very religious household but chose not to be as restrictive with my own son – and he also turned out to be ok. There is no right or wrong way to do something as long as each day brings you some motivation to keep going.

There is nothing special about me, but I have done some pretty special things. I've had lunch at the Governor's mansion in Raleigh. I've shaken hands with three United States Presidents (not because of anything I did but simply in the right place at the right time), and I have spoken at some very prestigious and important events. I was fortunate enough to work undercover narcotics during the height of the crack cocaine wars being waged in America (one of the most terrifying and exhilarating things I've ever done). I met and worked with some of the most brilliant, dedicated, and committed public servants that anyone could ever be fortunate enough to work with and learn from.

I got to teach the D.A.R.E. program for several years at the Morehead City Primary School (I mention the name of the school because I absolutely loved that experience) and was able to pay back my mother just a little for all the encouragement she gave me to teach. I was fortunate enough a couple of times to be in the right place to save a child's life and, unfortunately, not there in time to save others. I supervised and worked my way up to being the first female Chief of Police in a town in which I loved living and working.

The most important thing I've ever done in my life was to be the parent of a child, which God provided and helped me guide through his life. The only worry I have ever had that lasted more than a day or two is the same one that every parent has. I have worried about whether or not I have provided him with what he needs to be a good person, a good parent, and a good and contributing member of our society. I consider being a parent to be the most challenging and rewarding part of my life, and I understand what a great gift this child was to me and what a positive influence he has had in my life.

I bet as you were reading this, you commented (to yourself) that I am no better than you and certainly no smarter. You are right. I may be more fortunate and may have had more times than not where I have "been in the right place at the right time", but I am certainly no smarter or hard-working than you. So, please read the book and remember that you are as smart as me, as tough as me, and as capable of succeeding as anyone you've ever met or read about…

please remember those simple things and you will know all you ever need to know.

> *Always be proud of who you are and where you come from, because it's part of who you are.*

Key Takeaways and Action Items:

- View challenges as opportunities for growth rather than limitations. Focus on solutions, not obstacles, and invest in yourself even under difficult circumstances.
- Commit to lifelong learning. Invest time and effort into your education or skillset, regardless of immediate challenges.
- Be open to discovering your passion through experimenting with different paths.
- No matter how big or small, do your best to inspire and uplift others. Help create opportunities for people to grow.
- Adopt a mindset of perseverance. Face problems head-on with a belief in your ability to find solutions.
- If you're a parent, focus on being present and organized to create meaningful, lasting memories with your child(ren). Prioritize instilling values and life skills.
- Reflect on and appreciate how your background shapes you, but don't be afraid to create a life true to your own values and goals.
- Remind yourself of your strengths and capabilities. Believe you are as worthy and capable of success as anyone else.

- Adopt a "one step at a time" approach—focus on improving yourself daily, no matter what form that takes.
- Strive to leave a positive impact in your community or workplace, no matter how small the action may seem.

Remember

- Success isn't dependent on being "special" but on resilience, resourcefulness, and the courage to take the next step. The author invites readers to reflect, make changes in their lives, and continue striving toward their goals.

CHAPTER TWO

Success Comes To Those….

It does **NOT** come to those who wait, those born into wealth, or to hard-charging families. Nor does it come to those who simply work hard. There are plenty of hard-working and dedicated people who have jobs and live in poverty or near poverty, and regardless of how hard he or she works, nothing ever changes for them. WHY? There are also plenty of people (everyone) who have dreamed their entire lives about one particular thing, which would be a dream job or a dream life. Why can't they make that happen? Is it because they are bad people, and karma is repaying them for their former deeds? Is it because they were afraid to act quickly enough to get the prize at the end of the day? It is not because of any of those reasons. Sometimes, people simply need encouragement or pushing for them to feel like they can succeed. No brilliant answers to unanswered questions. Just encouragement and maybe an idea or two that he or she hasn't thought of or hasn't thought of as "being possible". Regardless of how much money you have, how smart you are, whom your parents are, or how hard your life is, no one (NO ONE) ever succeeds without help. It may not be much help and sometimes it might look like the opposite of help at the time, but every successful person has someone or something that propelled them forward.

However, if you work hard at the same job doing the same thing every day, nothing will change about your life. In everyone's life there is a story about opportunities missed. A job that you turned down because of a required move, or family obligations, fear, or a variety of reasons known only to you. What if I had majored in law instead of education? What if I had made better grades and dedicated myself to my education? What if I made that shot at the buzzer and gotten a scholarship to college? What if I had waited to have children until later, or had them earlier? What if I had married someone with the same goals and dreams as me? What if I had been born rich instead of poor? If I had an office job, I'd have more energy at the end of the day and could spend more time with the kids. Any of these questions sound familiar?

There are hundreds of "what ifs" that we can all use to justify our current situation. For me, I wonder what my life would have been like if I had been born different or born rich, done better and been focused in college, worked at a bigger department, followed my original plans? The reality is that it doesn't matter. None of those things matter because none of them helped me or hurt me in the decisions made in my life. None of those things mattered when I chose to succeed and refused to fail. More importantly for me, none of those things mattered when I refused to lose.

The things that I mentioned in chapter one, the ones that I felt strongly enough about to share with you; being a police officer, educating myself against seemingly insurmountable odds, and being a parent are all extremely important in my life. Not one of those things happened or were altered because of decisions made or challenges presented to me early in my life. Each of those things happened because I decided to overcome challenges and make my own decisions and control my own destiny as best as I could. It was never easy being a female police officer in a small town; especially one like me (you can google me to find out what that means if you're interested). It was also very hard to get an education as a working adult that lived basically "paycheck to paycheck". Parenting is never easy and deciding to put his life first before everything else in my life was a conscious decision that was not taken lightly nor made without repercussions. However, I did it and again, you and I are not that different. Trust me, if I can do it, anyone can do it. All you have to do is refuse to fail at what is important to you. It really is just that simple. I must say before moving on that being a parent is by far the most important thing you will ever do and failing at that job not only impacts your child but the entire society. We all must commit to raising our children rather than palming them off on others to raise and then complaining when they don't turn out the way we planned. (my rant on society's failures)

Key Takeaways and Action Items:

- Seek encouragement and guidance from others, and don't hesitate to offer support when you can.
- Take proactive steps to explore new paths or opportunities rather than staying in a stagnant position.
- Focus on the future, not the past. Use your experience to inform better decisions moving forward.
- Foster a mindset of perseverance, especially when facing challenges. Refuse to fail at what truly matters to you.
- Dedicate yourself wholeheartedly to important roles, such as being a parent, as they have far-reaching consequences.
- Success is a choice to persist, adapt, and take responsibility. Refuse to accept failure, and you can achieve what's most important.

CHAPTER THREE

What If?

I wonder all the time what my life how my life would be different if I had been born to rich parents that knew how to help me get through college or were able to help me get a good job. Then, reality sets in and I realize that if those things had happened, I would not be here and certainly would not have benefited from the hardships, love, and support that I had my whole life that made me who I am. It is important that we stop blaming others for our lack of success. Your parents did not prevent you from being successful nor did the fact that you didn't have the money or grades to get into Harvard or Duke. Those things did not stop you from doing anything you wanted to do… you did.

I grew up with a teenage mother and an orphaned father that will readily admit that they were not prepared to raise children but did the best that they could. I grew up poor but was perfectly healthy and had very involved parents. They did not have money to send me to Ivy league schools or to buy me new cars, but they did encourage me to believe in myself.

There was never a time in my life that I wasn't told that I would go to college. There was also never a time when anyone told me how I would get there. That, I had to figure out on my own, and I did. My parents always expected me to succeed because they expected me to behave, they expected me to study and get good grades, they expected me to be a good person, and as contradictory as it is today, they expected me to attend church and be a part of the Christian faith. I think all those things made me a strong, hardworking, polite person that knows the difference in right and wrong and knows the importance of having a strong and committed family. They never doubted that my sister or I would be successful because they expected us to be.

What if, I had given up on going to college and stayed home to work at the local Dollar General Store? Would I be a failure? Absolutely not, being a worker at a local store does not make you a failure any more than not being the CEO of a large corporation makes either of us a failure. What if instead of going to UNC-W, I had gone to NC State (which was my first choice, but Carolina was the first choice of my best friend, so we compromised and went to UNC-W)? Who knows what my life would be like today if I had taken different paths. The point is that I didn't choose either of those different paths. THE POINT IS, previous decisions do not matter and cannot stop you from succeeding today… absolutely can NOT stop you. What can stop you is using those decisions as an excuse for why you are not successful. Oh, if only I had gone to NC State then I could have been an engineer instead of a police officer… who cares where you went to school. What you did yesterday cannot be un-done but it also cannot stop you from doing something different today. Yesterday is gone… let it go and move on to today.

So, how do we succeed if we are born poor or don't have parents that encourage us? How do we reach our dreams without someone to help us? How do I get that job, that education, that business that I've always wanted? It's simple really. You just do it – and no, I'm not quoting a Nike commercial. Stop blaming others for your lack of success and stop using your former or current circumstances to stop you from succeeding! If you want something, go get it. It's really that simple.

Oh no, what if your credit is bad? What if you have three children that all need new shoes? What if your husband is not supportive and "won't let you" do what you want to do? Seriously, these are all just excuses and justifications for you not taking control of your life… stop listening to negative people and stop being negative. The first thing you need to do is stop listening to the negativity that surrounds us every day. If you live in negativity, you blame the world for your problems and you never change. Change is not easy, but it is possible, and it is all up to you.

I'm 5'0" Tall – And Want To Play In The WNBA

I've had many dreams throughout my life and many of them are just like yours. I wanted to play basketball and be the star. I wanted to make records and sell them to millions of people and watch them sing along with my songs on the radio as I rode down the street. I wanted to have a large family and watch the kids play outside while I wrote best-selling novels. None of those things came true… not one. Does that mean I failed to reach my dreams or that I am a failure? NO! I've always been an active person but at 5'2" (really more like 5'1") it is not really realistic to believe that I would be a basketball star in the WNBA. Doesn't mean that you can't do that if you're 5'2", but being realistic is important when choosing a dream to follow. Not only am I short (by any standards), but I am also not a great basketball player (I was however great in my backyard). Still my favorite sport but liking to play doesn't mean that I'll ever be great at it. Realistic goals are important.

Dreaming at 12 years old is also a little different than dreaming at 30, 40, or 50 years old too. Every single day after school, I went outside and played basketball for hours. Every time I made a great shot (they were all great in my head) I told myself that I could be a professional basketball player. Please keep in mind also that the WNBA did not exist at that time but still, I wanted to be a professional basketball player. I'd play out game situations in my head and using imaginary opponents and game clocks… always making the winning shot at the buzzer. I wouldn't trade those days for ones reading books about teaching or engineering or any topic that I could have used to start a real career. I love those memories and the fact that I always made the shot at the buzzer… and on those rare occasions when the ball rolled off the rim – I was always fouled and won the game at the free throw line with no time left on the clock.

There is a difference in dreaming and setting goals. Dreams are often confused with fantasies. It is a fantasy to play in the WNBA, but it is not really a dream of mine. If it were a dream, then I would have committed every waking minute to making it come true. I made the basketball team in high school and once in college, but the fact was that I was not that good at it. I am one of those people that can do almost anything, (except bowling and skiing… can't do either of those things) but I'm not great at doing them. So, all those imaginary basketball games played out in my backyard were only important in that they provided me with a way to burn some energy, be a hero even if only in my own head and helped me realize that sometimes fantasizing about something is fun and fun is important. I enjoy thinking about the time I spent playing basketball in the yard and I believe that all children need to be allowed to do what makes them happy, whether they're good at it or not. As long as it is fun for them. They will figure out soon enough that they are not the next Mia Hamm or LeBron James, just like I did. Side note, if my parents had pushed me to play a sport to make them happy, I probably would not have these fun memories… (another rant about society).

Playing music is my favorite pastime and makes me forget about all the problems of the world. It truly makes me happy to pick up a guitar and play a song and when I was younger and dreaming about being rich and famous, playing that guitar was my solace. However, it is hard to be a rock star, and I wasn't willing to do all the things necessary to make that happen. Didn't stop me from dreaming about it, but I didn't want to travel, didn't want to live in someone's garage, and can't stand rejection.

So, rock star wasn't a realistic dream for me either. Am I a failure because I gave up on that dream? I don't think so because I took great pleasure from playing that guitar and writing crazy songs while I dreamed and took myself away from the reality of my world at that point in my life. That fantasy world provided a great deal of peace for me during my teenage years and gives me pleasure now that nothing else can bring. So, that dream helped make me who I am, but again I wasn't dedicated enough to the dream to make it happen. So, much like playing basketball, playing the guitar and writing songs simply provided me with an outlet and time away from the family.

I spent many afternoons with a guitar and my dog sitting alongside of Deep River in Guilford County, North Carolina playing until my fingers were raw. My dog (Tinker) howled as I played and sang. He quite enjoyed the run from the house to our favorite spot along the riverbank, but not so much the guitar and singing (should've been a clue that rock star wasn't going to happen). Again, based on my lack of willingness to sacrifice my time and my fear of rejection, being a professional singer was not for me.

Can you sing or play the guitar? Do you write songs? Are you good at it or simply enjoy it? Doesn't matter really if you're good at it as long as it makes you happy. I believe that music is the window into our very soul, that children should be introduced to it, and that it should be a part of every school day and every day around the house. How often do you hear a song on the radio from your childhood that takes you back to those days? That one song appearing unexpectedly can change your entire day. Remember, what touches your heart and/or soul today may provide inspiration, motivation, and spur action for you tomorrow.

I have very fond memories of my mother playing the radio and singing along while she did household chores. She sang all the time, and we often sang along with her and when I hear those songs (both rock n roll and gospel) I remember that moment in time, and it makes me remember how the house smelled, what we were doing at that moment, and how happy we were. Those memories make me happy, and I can't imagine not having those moments. I have great memories of singing in the children's choir at church and hearing gospel songs during church. Those songs and those moments are very much a part of who I am. Watching guitar players and piano players at church mesmerized me… probably much more than the actual sermon.

So, don't rob yourself or others of that joy and potential for greatness. Sing when you feel like it and even when you don't. Listen to an "oldies but goodies" radio station once in a while and recapture some of your youthful memories and dreams. Life can be just that simple. Happiness is a great motivator, so never deny yourself things that make you happy because of what someone else thinks or because you are good at it. Sing loud and if you can't carry a tune, sing louder and laugh while you do it.

> *If something makes you happy, smile and keep doing it.*

Key Takeaways and Action Items:

- Take ownership of your life choices and focus on actionable steps to achieve your goals.
- Appreciate and leverage foundational values instilled by your upbringing, however modest they may seem.
- Set realistic goals while still allowing yourself the joy of dreaming and pursuing passions.
- Avoid dwelling on past decisions or "what if" scenarios; focus on the present and future.
- Seek positive influences and eliminate negativity that could hinder your progress.
- Reassess your dreams and goals periodically to ensure they remain aligned with your current reality and passions.

CHAPTER FOUR

So, How Do I Plan To Succeed?

Sometimes, success is relevant to you and your situation. For example, success for me is being financially able to live comfortably, to make my child's life easier than mine was (which is probably a mistake), and to be able to help other people that are not as fortunate as I have been. So, am I successful if I don't have lots of money and didn't realize any of my childhood dreams? Am I successful if I'm happy and comfortable in my own life? Yes, but I didn't wake up this morning with a happy life. It took a lot of work to make me happy.

I fell into my job as a police officer and immediately fell in love with the profession. I called my mother after being on the job for about a week and told her that I was going to retire from this department and this job because I couldn't imagine doing anything else.. ever! That became my dream, and I made that dream come true. Why? How does a dream happen by accident? I found a job that made me feel needed and made me feel like I was doing something important. I have never felt like I was important to the job but that the job was important and that I was a part of something much bigger than me. Not a professional athlete or a rock star but a police officer. Wow, my dreams were all over the place and I am still dreaming.

I may have found my calling when I became a police officer, but I was never satisfied with the profession and still am not satisfied. I immediately wanted to change everything about the profession I loved so much. I thought the officers were too robotic and not involved enough. I thought they were racists, sexists, and overbearing and I quickly realized that I wanted to make a difference in this profession. Making changes in a paramilitary organization that is male dominated and consumed with keeping things the same is not an easy task. So, how did I make changes and succeed in this field? I planned out my career, I stayed inspired to reach my goals, I maintained my motivation and faith in the mission, and I worked very hard every day. If you lose faith in yourself, you will not succeed. There is a difference between getting anxious about the mission and losing faith. There are lots of days that I've been anxious but there has never been a day when I've lost faith in myself. Why?

I've maintained faith in myself by believing in what I was doing and in my goals. If I continued to maintain a dream or goal of being a rock star but never committed to working hard enough to get there, it would be easy to lose faith in myself and my abilities. I knew and have always known that if I continued to chip away at bad policies, bad hiring and retention practices, and rigid restrictions that I could succeed at making changes in my department. I also knew that if I got the right education and training, worked harder than everyone else, (yes, ladies you will have to outwork everyone else) and stayed true to my own morals and ethics that I could succeed in this profession and in this department. I never lost faith in myself.

So, how does that apply to my life today or to your life? Today, I am writing a book (which is something that I have wanted to do my entire life) and all sorts of thoughts run through my head. For instance, is this another example of me playing basketball with imaginary opponents or writing and singing rock songs? Who is going to read this, how will I get it published, and what good will it do for someone else? All very important questions, especially when I have just spent a great deal of time talking about my youthful adventures on the farm (did I mention that I grew up on a farm?).

I recently retired from the job that I have loved for 29 years. My biggest fear about retirement was being alone and away from the people that I have both served with and served for a large majority of my life. Lots of things run through your mind when you prepare for retirement – most of them related to fear. Fear that you haven't done enough in the job. Fear that you really won't be missed. Fear that you will be bored and miserable and most importantly fear that your life will lose meaning without serving others.

I tell you these things because fear of change is natural and an important part of life. That's what keeps us from walking out of every job we have the first time something happens that we don't like. It's what keeps us from jumping off cliffs without knowing what is at the bottom of the cliff. It is also what helps us plan for the future and face all of our fears about change. I realized early in the retirement process (which started about three years ago) that my life was going to drastically change. I also realized that I needed to be prepared for those changes and find ways to challenge myself.

My dream now is to help other women achieve success whether that means being a good mother, wife, and friend or whether it means opening and running a multi-million-dollar business. Both of those jobs (yes being a wife, mother, and friend is quite a challenging job) are challenging and both are vital to our existence. We need good mothers and sometimes we need someone to tell us that we are doing a good job when others are too busy to notice. We also need new businesses opened and properly managed to provide a living in our communities and for our families.

My dream now is to help myself stay relevant by helping others realize what their dreams are and how to turn those dreams into a reality. Am I a little intimidated by this change? Yes, I am. Not because it's that much of a daunting task but because it is so important. Because you and I are not very different from each other, I know how scared you are sometimes and how much you want to succeed. I know how many nights you can't sleep because you're trying to figure out how to buy your kid a new pair of shoes and wondering why you can't manage your money. I know how many days you find yourself wondering why someone else took your idea and made a million dollars with it. I've been there and I've had those same thoughts and dreams.

Turning your nightmares into an attainable dream will not happen because you think about it all the time. Being a successful mother, businesswoman, teacher, or friend takes work and sacrifice but not more than you can give. Maybe more than you are willing to give but not more than you CAN give. Let's talk a little about what you have to do to be successful at anything and everything once you decide it is important to you.

When the storm is coming, prepare.

Planning

I have always been one to set very high goals and too many goals at one time. In order to continue to succeed and not stalemate, it was important to plan every step of the way. I had to plan my education and make sure that I fought through the overwhelming desire to quit. I quit college and left UNC-W without a degree (UNC-W by the way, was the best decision for me, even over my beloved NC State). That is a hard statement for me to make, but I made up for it by going on to finish a Ph.D. It is embarrassing to me to admit that I quit college and did not graduate from the university that meant so much to me. In a life filled with so many fun and worthy adventures and successes, my time at UNC-Wilmington will always be some of the best times of my life. It is where I learned that I could live on my own, where I became confident in myself, and where I learned that there were other people like me in the world. Yet, I left there without finishing.

Failure, right? I left high school and attended UNC-W with scholarships and grants and was expected to do well in college. I continued to be met with high expectations from my entire family as the first of 27 grandkids to attend college. The fact was, however, that I did not want to be in college because I didn't know what I wanted to do. I felt like I was wasting everybody's time and money because I knew I would not be a teacher. Life has a funny way of bringing up old memories because just last night, I had a conversation with my son about what he wanted to do with his life. He very seriously said to me that he has no idea what he wants to do and if I ask him again in 30 minutes or two weeks, he will not know then either. I remember that feeling from college but the difference is that I was not strong enough at the time to admit it and he is… so, maybe me quitting college was a way for me to understand and be understanding of his position in life. I certainly have no room to judge him or scold him because he is much stronger at 19 than I was.

I do not consider myself a failure because I quit college (maybe a little disappointed that none of the degrees hanging on the wall have UNC-W written on them). I look back at that time and those challenges and realize that each decision made led me to where I am today. I made some good decisions and made lots of really bad ones, but each one forced me to alter my path just enough to lead me here. Writing a book about success – what a journey this has been and what a challenge it still is… back to the topic of planning.

So, planning to finish school while I worked a police officer's rotating schedule was important and required a great deal of planning. I had to plan classes, time off, homework time, family time, and leisure time. Each of which is important to everyday life and each of which was tricky to schedule. I worked many nights getting off at 7 am and drove two hours away to take classes. I stayed up most of the night writing and doing homework and often went to work with 3-4 hours' sleep because it was important to spend time with my family. Planning each of these activities was vital to my success.

My son was born on the first day of my first graduate class so obviously planning is not my biggest strength. I am a person that needs timelines and deadlines and when I signed up for graduate school, I set the finish point at 18 months. I planned each day like I was planning my graduation and there were many days that I did not reach my goal – but there were many days that I did everything I needed to get done. I will tell you that if you ask anyone that knows me, they will tell you that I am not a very organized or planned person. I am known for being a procrastinator and flying by the seat of my pants kind of person – which is true. However, it is a planned flight.

I plan late nights that no one else sees and I plan to neglect this so I can focus on that. I plan for chaos because that is when I do my best work... I like deadlines and timelines. If I know what I expect to get done this week, I will get it done. No excuses – get it done. If I don't, the only person being let down is me and I am important to me and don't want to let myself down. Did you catch that? I am important to me, and you should be important to you. What you want to do and what you want to achieve is important and should be considered a priority. I'm not telling you to put yourself ahead of everything and everyone in your life, but I am telling you to plan for your own success by realizing that what you want is important.

PLAN everything and stick to the plan. It is not necessary to plan your life to the point of misery, but it is important to have a plan and realize that things happen to alter the plan from time to time. That doesn't mean that the plan changes or stops being important. It simply means that today didn't go as planned but that doesn't mean that the week won't or if the week is difficult don't give up on the month. One bad week doesn't make a bad month any more than a bad month ruins an entire year. Plan to meet your goals.

Planning can be as simple picking one night, or one day, or two hours for you spend working on yourself this week. For example, most people don't work out because they can't find the time. Plan the time. Plan to walk around the block every day at 5:15 when you get home from work and before you sit down. Plan to do some yoga on the Wii while the baby takes a nap. Plan to walk up and down the stairs at home 10 times today and just get it done. At the end of the day when you accomplished that goal, smile and tell yourself that this is the beginning of change.

Plan to start school and start researching online classes or go to the community college and talk to someone about taking classes. Have you ever done that? The people that work at the community college in your county (or city) are extremely helpful and many of them started off by doing exactly what you're doing – talking to someone about getting started. You can't finish if you don't get started.

I certainly did not do things in the right order and never did anything the easy way. I am still trying to finish a Ph.D. and financing my life away, to get that done so, please don't think this is simple. Have you ever heard that everything in life worth having is worth working for? Well, it is worth working for and that all starts with the plan. The best approach for me to have (and keep) throughout my life is to remember that every plan (even the best laid plans) gets messed up sometimes. My son being born on the first day of my first graduate class was horrifying to me – and the best thing that has ever happened to me at the same time. So, what does that tell us about a plan? Plans change but don't lose sight of the end goal. If you can dream it, you can make it happen!

Ride the rails… just once!

Key Takeaways and Action Items:

- Reflect on what success looks like for you and align your goals with this vision.
- Create a detailed roadmap that includes achievable steps for your goals, ensuring to balance personal and professional aspects of your life.

- Believe in your abilities and your mission, even during times of anxiety or fear. Trust that consistent effort will lead to achievement.
- Anticipate and accept that change is inevitable. Use planning to alleviate fear and smooth transitions.
- Consider how you can assist others in achieving their dreams. Success is not just personal—it's also about contributing to others' lives.
- Remember that sacrifices and setbacks are part of the process. Stay focused, work hard, and adapt as needed.

CHAPTER FIVE

Be Inspired

What does that even mean? Be inspired? I can tell you what it means to me. Every day I am inspired to do something positive that day. Who inspires me and what am I inspired to do? It depends really. Sometimes people and their stories inspire me. For example, I worked with several people that struggle every day to get up and come to work because of a variety of problems. Most of their problems are self-inflicted and could be avoided or changed quite simply but yet they never do what is necessary to change. However, they continue to come to work and, in most cases, come with a smile or at least willing to help others through their struggles. This inspires me, because by all accounts my life is good and if they can work and function in their families with their problems, surely, I can be positive and accomplish something today.

Other days, I am inspired by what I read or what I hear from a total stranger. If I talk to someone that tells me their story of success, I allow myself to be inspired by their story. Did you catch that? I allow myself to be inspired. I don't wish I were as successful as that person, or as pretty, or as rich. I don't secretly wonder why they deserved to be that happy or successful. I simply allow myself to be inspired by their story and sometimes their struggles as they complete their journey to success. Very often we spend too much time wondering why they are more successful than we are, or why they married whom they married rather than simply listening to their story. Every story has a dark side, and every successful person has struggled in some way to get to where they are. Stop looking for flaws and be happy for them and most importantly stop finding excuses for why they succeed and why you don't.

Reading offers a great source of inspiration and if you're anything like me, you don't have hours to read inspirational stories every day. So, do what I do and find a devotional or a website that offers simple inspirational quotes. I like simple quotes that make me think – you know like "ask not what your country can do for you" kind of quotes. I actually started sending quotes to my son every day when he was in the ninth grade. Sometimes he responds but most of the time he simply reads it and ignores me, but my point has always been that we never know what will inspire us today. Some days, he came home and said that he liked the quote that I sent him that day, and that made me smile.

I have spent a great deal of time talking and listening to people throughout my career and have taken great comfort in watching others succeed. I have listened to young women tell me why they will be the first female president of the United States (J.M.) and I believe them. I recently began sending one of those young women inspirational quotes and last Thursday she sent me one back. It said, "you can spend all your time sleeping with your dreams, or you can wake up and chase them". I thought that was a great quote and was tickled that she sent it to me. This young mother of two small children is an amazing woman with many talents. I believe that she can be president one day but whether she will, depends on her desire to overcome her fears (if she reads this she will say that she has no fears – but we all do).

A quote that inspires me today and makes me feel energetic or positive may not inspire me tomorrow so tomorrow, I will find something else to inspire me. I am constantly looking for something to inspire me, but my main inspiration always comes from my search. For example, if I am looking for a quote that inspires me and see a child laughing uncontrollably or hear a coworker laughing loud enough that it fills the hallways, that can certainly be an unexpected or unintended inspiration. Take inspiration from wherever it comes from – don't let yourself be discouraged because you didn't find a quote or hear a story or speak to an inspirational person today. If all else fails, look within.

I can inspire myself by doing simple things. Simple things like walking the dog or mopping the floor when I had no plans to do it. Spur of the moment accomplishments inspire me to do more. I am by nature a positive person so inspiration can come easily to me. However, I have a dark side (as do most of you) and there are days when Mother Theresa herself would have a hard time inspiring me. So what happens on those days? I go about my day and allow myself to be inspired and more importantly, never denying myself happiness or inspiration when it comes unexpectedly.

There are days when I look outside through a window in my office and wish I was out there, and that usually motivates me to finish what I'm doing. Some days, when it's cloudy or raining outside, I am happy to be inside and sometimes I'm inspired to work hard because it's raining so I don't have to work so hard on the sunny days. There are days when seeing the wind blow through the trees or hearing a bird sing inspires or awakens a sense of happiness in me. I am thankful for those simple things and try very hard to find them when I am feeling down.

I have a friend that was critically injured last year and nearly died. He has said to me many times in the past year that he now notices things that he never looked twice at before. He notices a tree and says out loud that the tree is pretty and often wonders why he is noticing the tree. Then he remembers how close he came to dying and how much he wants to live and enjoy everything and everyone in his life while he still can. Be inspired by the things around you and never be afraid to embrace whatever it is that inspires you. Remember the "oldies but goodies" radio station? Let music, or nature, or the quiet inspire you to change one thing about today that makes it better than yesterday. Small changes can make a big difference.

Around the bend, there is new and different light… Find it!

Key Takeaways and Action Items:

- **Start every day with inspiration** – Find a quote, story, or moment to set a positive tone for your day.
- Remember that even successful individuals face struggles. Use their stories as encouragement, not as a point of comparison.
- Make it a habit to acknowledge small joys like the sight of a tree, a bird singing, or the sound of laughter.
- Make one small improvement to your day that sets it apart from yesterday—no matter how simple.

- Even on tough days, allow yourself to notice small moments that spark joy or positivity.
- Share inspirational moments or quotes with friends or family, creating a ripple effect of positivity.

CHAPTER SIX

Motivation

How do I stay motivated? For me, timelines and deadlines keep me motivated. I need deadlines, and without them, I tend to procrastinate and slough off, causing my plan to take a backseat to wasted days or time spent complaining about a lack of time to get things done. Motivation, like inspiration, often comes from unexpected places. I am motivated to work hard because I have an important job. If you are a mother or parent of a child, you have the most important job in the world and while some days are better than others, your child should motivate you to be a great parent. That child, your family, and our society depend on you being a great parent.

I had a conversation recently with a young lady who is struggling with issues related to her parents. She desperately wants children but is afraid that she will be the kind of parent that she has had her entire life; a bad parent. We discussed parenting and while I am certainly no expert in parenting, I have studied lots of parents over the past 29 years and have seen some great ones and some terrible ones. The most important thing about parenting is to recognize the importance of the job and to work every day at spending time with your children and making them feel loved, protected, and confident. Recognizing your fears and working hard to not repeat the mistakes of the past is such a wonderful statement about your future. I am confident that this young woman will be a great mother because she is motivated to be great.

I am motivated by failure and that simply means that I work hard so I don't fail at my daily tasks. I can't stand failure whether it's related to work, home, school, or life and that motivates me to keep going. I don't like failing at things that matter or those that don't. What does that mean? If I decide that I am going to wash my car today and the day gets away from me, I am not happy that I failed to get a simple thing done that literally takes 15 minutes. Does that matter? No, but I don't like failing so it matters to me. I don't like to fail at things that matter such as job tasks or meeting a specific goal associated with something that means something to me. Even though I didn't make it to the WNBA, I'm still very competitive and like winning much more than losing so I do what I need to do to win.

What motivates you? Is it hard for you to get motivated to read a book, to write a paper, to take a class? How about losing weight? That seems to be hard for us all and as we age it becomes even harder (I'm short, getting older by the day, and tend to be a little fluffy so I understand). So how do we motivate ourselves and/or how do we seek motivation? You seek motivation by allowing yourself to be motivated by whatever makes you feel better. For instance, if something happens and it makes you feel good then you should smile. If it makes you sad, cry. Can sadness motivate you? Of course it can. If you see a sad movie about childhood illness or homelessness and it motivates you to do something, then get off the couch and do it. If something motivates you, get up and do something. It really is that simple.

Motivation comes in the form of self-discipline. If you want to stop smoking, then stop smoking by doing whatever is necessary to stop. If that means changing your work habits, your friends, your family time, then change it. Each cigarette that you skip will motivate you to skip the next one. If you want to become a runner, then run a block today then tomorrow remember how good you felt after you ran the block and go run 2 blocks. Allow small accomplishments to motivate the next one. It is really that simple. Life is not difficult to figure out. We blame our failure or lack of motivation on so many things that we begin to justify our failures. Stop blaming and start moving forward – one step at a time. Just keep moving.

Sometimes, reading a self-help book can motivate you just as listening to Joyce Myers deliver a message can motivate you. Sometimes, knowing that another January 1st is coming motivates you to set new goals for the year. Sometimes, we find it difficult to find anything that motivates us and feel helpless. So, what happens on those days and what happens when those days turn into weeks or months? Seriously, how did I go from being a serious (ok, somewhat serious) runner to being 20 pounds overweight? Laziness? Depression?

Not necessarily, life just gets in the way sometimes and we take a break. It's just that simple. However, when that happens it is important to snap out of it and get moving for your sake. Each of us have to find what motivates us and to constantly search for those things because like I said earlier, what motivates or inspires us today might not work tomorrow. How many "new year's resolutions" have you kept in your lifetime? Stop setting ridiculous goals and take one day at a time… motivate yourself today!

Sometimes, a gentle push is a good thing.

Hard Work

It is easy to be lazy and blame others or our circumstances for our failure, but it is not as easy to take responsibility for our own life. Knowing where you come from and understanding why you are the way you are is important, but using that knowledge to move forward is more important. I was a poor child of teenage parents, but I did not become a teenage parent of a poor child because I wanted to do something different in my life. Being a product of your environment requires that you give in to those around you rather than taking responsibility for your own life.

My sister and I both graduated from college, and I am very proud of that fact. We did not come from a family of college graduates and neither of us got rich or famous because we graduated from college. However, education is something that no one can take away from me and that makes it very important to me. My sister by the way is the smart one in the family that has all the artistic talent, organizational skills, and ability to see beauty in things that I might refer to as junk. I'm not sure how that happened but it's true. She has overcome many obstacles in her life, as we all have, but I am very often motivated by her because I know her story and exactly what she has had to overcome. If you know my sister, please don't tell her that I said nice things about her. She knows that she is smarter than me but she doesn't know that I know it too.

Are you strong enough to overcome your past? Yes, you are! We all are, and we all should be proud of where we came from as we are leaving it behind. I will not be ashamed of who I am because it took a lot to get me here and every single part of my life played a role in who I have become. However, while I am proud of my background, I will not be defined by it. I want to be defined by what I am today and what I will become tomorrow. I can be whatever I choose to be and so can you.

I am by nature a very shy person and most of my adult life have had to force myself to speak to large groups of people. I pretend I am someone else when I speak – seriously, I pretend that I am not shy and know what I am talking about. I refuse to be crippled by my shyness and force myself to speak. While I am speaking, I pray that no one sees my knees shaking and that the quiver in my voice when I first start is forgotten before I finish. I have developed a plan for all my speeches and never deviate from the plan. I cannot use notes (slight dyslexia and extreme nerves) because I am afraid that I will lose my place and be unable to recover. Instead, I always begin with a quote that I can memorize about whomever or whatever the topic of the speech is. I follow the quote with simple stories about the topic that I can talk about like I am talking to a friend. Then, finally I end the speech with another quote hoping that what I said in the middle makes sense, or that the ending quote was the only thing they remember. I stick to this plan because of fear of failure. Important people and important events deserve confident speakers, and this plan enables me to perform and allows me to overcome my fear.

Hard work means different things to different people but to me it means taking on challenges and not leaving until the job is done. There were many times in my career when my shift was over long before the job was done. I always admired those that stayed until the job was done and always wondered how someone could leave the job undone. There are workers and there are clock-watchers. If you pay attention, you will see that the workers usually are those that get the promotion, the pay raise, or the acclaim. The clock-watchers? They're usually the complainers that spend their days whining about how unfair life is and how the workers are suck ups, boot lickers, butt kissers, etc. Have you met these people? They are miserable and try their best to make you miserable. They are the kind that respond to "good morning" with a hardy "what's so good about it?". They're the ones that leave early for lunch and come back late. They clean their desk ten minutes before their day ends in preparation for their exit.

I always envisioned their home to be a place full of miserable people who rely on the misery of others to make them smile. Hard work is just what it seems like it would be – it is hard. If you are a worker, confident, and stay with the task until it is finished, you will succeed. If you quit when things get difficult, you will always be a quitter, a whiner, or answer every "good morning" with a "what's so good about it?" Don't be that person, hard work won't kill you, but it will help you succeed.

Even if you feel boxed in, cut through the water like you own it!

Your Plan

If you decide that you want to do something, make a realistic plan to get it done. If this means getting a four-year degree and you are a parent of a 3-year-old child, then don't plan on getting a degree in four years. Develop a realistic plan and then go to work. As simple as that sounds, that is all you need to begin your move. Hard work is not something you should fear, rather it is something that you should look forward to and relish. Hard work will come naturally when you are committed to your plan of achieving your new goals. It does not mean that you neglect your family or abandon your own life. Hard work simply means that you do what is necessary to succeed. Remember, no one needs to know your plan unless you want them to. Let them wonder how you get everything done and marvel at your accomplishments. Remember me saying earlier that most (ok, all) of my friends will tell you that I am unorganized and not a good planner? I plan my life and make my life happen while others are sleeping or not paying attention because my plan is just that. It is mine.

Success is also not a word that you should fear. Success should be viewed as small steps toward your goal whether that goal is a four-year degree, a family, or a new business. If success is taken in small steps, then is does not become a daunting task. For instance, let's say that you want to open a new business and are not sure what you want to do. Research lots of businesses and business opportunities and you may be surprised at the opportunities available to you. Find a business that is already established or start your own but don't fear success, embrace it.

What if the business requires a huge down payment or a bank loan? So, what if it does? What happens if you ask that the down payment be lowered? If they say no, will it physically hurt you? No, so why not ask? I recently purchased a piece of property for a business that was priced at 500 thousand dollars and the down payment was $100,000 dollars. Remember that I was a police chief in a small town with a kid in college. I did not have $100,000. I desperately wanted this property and this business though and was determined to follow my own advice and figure it out. I went to see a friend of mine that had started several businesses over the years (some successful and some very un-successful) and asked him for advice.

The advice that he gave me was very simple. He said, "if you want this, then get over yourself and your weird sense of pride and ask the man to lower the down payment". Simple advice not worded very nice but brilliant advice for me. I did (do) have a weird sense of pride and was terrified to ask him to lower that down payment. But I did it and he agreed and also financed the property making the payment something that I can afford (as long as I don't intend to eat – every day).

This was a very big decision for me for many reasons but very simply put, I have never been a person that was over financed, and I was also very close to retirement. I have always told my son to want things that he has the money to pay for. I bought him a boat for his 14th birthday and paid for it in 18 months. I bought him a new car for his 16th birthday and paid for it in 18 months (so I could also afford to send him to college). I am a planner, and a saver verses a spender who panics when birthdays or Christmas gets here. I always have a pot of money put away for such events – all while making a very modest living at the police department. Trying to overcome those days of childhood when my parents struggled and listening to them try to figure out how to pay bills and send us to school. I watched my father work very hard to provide for us, and he did a great job of doing that. He also did a great job of teaching me how to work. My mother did a great job of providing a happy home for us and making sure we knew how to both work and enjoy our lives.

I also spoke to another good friend about this purchase and told her that I felt like I was about to jump off a cliff without a parachute. After telling me several times about how crazy I was (am) she told me to jump because I have always landed on my feet before. I realized while I was talking to her that she was right and that I wasn't really afraid, I was just nervous because I was going into debt when I was supposed to be retiring and enjoying my life. This particular friend tells me quite often how crazy I am but then always encourages me to keep jumping. We all need friends like her.

For me, enjoying life means being challenged, and this purchase was important to me. Getting a Ph.D. is also important to me and probably the most expensive thing I've done in my life, but remember me saying earlier that I am important to me? I wanted this property and this degree and while I have been saving and pinching every penny I made over the past 20 years, I have done very little for me. So, I jumped off the cliff and am sitting in the office writing, looking out at the water – still wondering how I got the courage to take this leap of faith and what it is about me that makes me think I can pull this off.

Back to you… What about a bank loan? Most of us have credit issues, nothing of value to vouch for the loan, and no family member that will co-sign. I am willing to bet you that if you do your research and find something that you are passionate about doing, you can write a business plan and get the loan. Remember when I said that I asked the owner of this property to lower the cash down payment? He also financed the loan, making it available to me when it would have been difficult (to say the least) if I had gone to a bank. If you don't ask, you won't know what the possibilities are, and you may be surprised at the answer.

A few years ago, I was the only one working in my family and we had a baby to feed and to hopefully put through college someday. We followed the same approach as I just mentioned and began to research available businesses in the area that would support our goals. We found a small seafood market and began discussions with the owner about buying the business. He wanted to sell and was asking a reasonable amount for the business. But, like many of you, I had no collateral other than my house and no money in the bank. So, the same friend that told me to get over my weird sense of pride sent me to a banker that he knew, and we negotiated the loan for the business. WOW… it was just that simple. The seafood market was a success and was the result of asking the right questions and not being afraid to "jump off the cliff". In all fairness, I did get the loan for the business and the business was more than just a success, it was a phenomenal success. However, I did not run the business and am not responsible for the success other than procuring the money. My business partner ran the business and with no formal training, little education, and no experience turned an underperforming seafood market into a tremendous success. So, the moral to that story is that sometimes it is necessary to combine your strengths with those of others to get what you want.

Not everyone has a friend who has business experience and/or a friend who is a banker. Not everyone has a friend who tells you how crazy you are and then encourages you to be even crazier. That doesn't matter at all. I am a cop and certainly not a business person and I am also very shy which can be mistaken for a lack of confidence in some people. Fortunately, (or unfortunately) my shyness makes me overcompensate and I often come across as over confident (or arrogant) sometimes as I try not to cry in the corner. The point of this conversation is that even without those friends who encourage you to jump, you can do whatever you want to do whether it is a business or going back to school.

I have dedicated my life to helping people like you reach for and grab with both hands what you have been dreaming about all your life. Plenty of people like me will share their stories with you, and hopefully, something in that story will encourage you or help you get started. Remember, you can't finish if you never start.

If you research, plan, and go to work to make your goal a reality then you will succeed at whatever you decide to do. If you decide to lose weight, approach it with the same zeal as you would a new business. Research it, develop a plan, and make the commitment to get it done. Why do you need to research and plan to lose weight? Because no matter what you decide to do, it is going to take hard work to get it done. Decide how to do what you want to do and work hard to get it done.

The two stories about buying the seafood market and the property for the business may sound like fairy tales and like the money and contracts were easy to get. Neither of those things are true. Remember me saying that I am a planner and a saver of money? Borrowing money for the seafood market required that I put up our house as collateral and also required that I worked a full-time job, worked part time at the market, and spent every waking minute with my son. The hard work and long hours never bothered me but borrowing money nearly caused me to have a nervous breakdown. I need to be in control and when you owe money some of that control is taken away from you. The moral to the story is that I took the risk, I worked hard, and never forgot what was most important to me (my son, in case I haven't made that clear before) and I jumped off the cliff. If you don't jump, you'll never enjoy the feeling of being free – free from fear, free from your own self-inflicted pain, and free from financial burdens.

I talked about my fantasies as a child and about how unrealistic they were based on my commitment level. I also mentioned that once I found something I was passionate about, I worked very hard to succeed at my mission to make a change in law enforcement. It is not enough for you to work as hard as everyone else. It is necessary for you to work harder than every single person you know. If you want to get a degree in 4 years, then work harder than any 18-year-old kid you know and get it done. If you want to start a business, then find out how to do it and then work like a person on a mission to catch their next breath and get it done.

I have started a business from scratch, I have taken over an existing business, and I have worked for the government. Each is hard in a different way, but each is also very exciting. If you create a dream and see it realized, then you have done something that no one else has done. You made your dream come true.

Don't be afraid to fly alone.

Key Takeaways and Action Items:

- Write down what motivates you the most. Is it avoiding failure, succeeding for your family, or personal growth? Use this as a focal point when you feel uninspired.
- Break long-term objectives into smaller, achievable milestones. For example, if quitting smoking, focus on skipping one cigarette at a time.
- Hold yourself accountable. Avoid procrastination and blaming external circumstances. Keep moving, even if progress is slow.
- Commit to finishing tasks, even when they become difficult. Avoid behaviours typical of "clock-watchers" or complainers.
- Reflect on what motives or strategies currently work for you. Adjust and refine those strategies over time to stay aligned with your goals.
- Approach challenges (e.g., public speaking or life obstacles) with consistent plans and incremental steps. Remember, temporary struggles don't define your future.

CHAPTER SEVEN

What If I Fail?

So what? What if you plan and dedicate yourself to this dream and work as hard as you can possibly work, and it fails? It doesn't matter – at all. Failure does not mean that you didn't make a lot of money or that your business failed. Failure means that you give up on your dream. Thomas Edison held 1,093 patents in his lifetime, but we are most familiar with the light bulb and the telegraph. Did you know that he invented the phonograph and the electric generator? Many of his inventions were very successful and extremely important to our way of life today. However, many of his inventions are unknown. Is that because they were unsuccessful? Absolutely not! Most of his patents are very successful and unknown to us because we either haven't needed the invention or simply haven't read about the connection between him and the invention. If he had given up on his dream, we'd all be reading this by candlelight in a dark room.

There are countless stories of actors, scientists, singers, and other famous and successful people that worked tirelessly for years before making the one decision that changed his or her life. How many times have you heard actors and actresses talk about working as waiters and waitresses to pay bills while they struggled to get an acting job? Each has a story involving rejection, poverty, and tireless pursuit of his or her dream. Doctors have stories of eating peanut butter sandwiches and working 36-hour shifts while in medical school before they graduated and started their practice.

What stories do you have of hard work and endless pursuit of your dream? Have you ever pursued a dream? What did you do to make sure you achieved your dream? Have you sacrificed your time, your money, your job? How can I expect you to give up what you have to get something new? If you are not willing to give up what you have now, you will never have something new or anything better. The same events lead to the same results. If you never change your ways, you will never change your results and sometimes sacrificing what you care about now is necessary to get what you dream about.

The point of this chapter is not to give up. That's it, nothing else. Just don't give up no matter how long it takes or what you have to sacrifice to get it. (Don't sacrifice your morals, ethics, or family for any dream) Many great people are only successful after their youth is gone. Remember Paula Deen? She became successful in her fifties and continues to gain popularity today. Paula Deen is a Southern woman who was a single mother with a goal of providing for her children. She did it because she refused to fail and not because she was smarter than you or even a better cook. She refused to quit searching for the right job, the right location, the right recipe that made her famous and she eventually found them all.

I watched a webinar recently (conducted by Simon Sinek) titled the Law of Diffusion of Innovation. Mr. Sinek talks a great deal about success and failure but what I took away from that webinar was much more than the difference between success and failure. For example, he talked about knowing why you are doing what you are doing before you determine what and how you are going to do it. Why is this important to me? It's important because there are a lot of people right now that want to be an author, consultant, and someone that helps women achieve their goals. That's what I want to do. There are also a lot of people out there who want to use the internet, do seminars, and conduct training on all those things. That's the how of this project. Most importantly, it is the why that matters the most.

I want to help women because no one else does. No one helps women who have children realize their dreams. No one thinks it is important that women are strong and confident enough to walk into a bank and ask for a bank loan to start a new business. I do. It's just that simple yet it was a brilliant awakening for me. Most people want to make money doing these things, but I want you to be successful. I don't need money – I like money just like you, but I have enough money to live and do the things that make me happy. (saying "I don't need money" implies that I have money, which is not true, I just have enough). So, I am doing this because I want you to be successful and not only does that make me happy, but it will also make me successful. Because in the end, the "why" is more important than the "what or how" of doing business.

Are you opening a clothing shop because you want to make money or because there is a need in your community for that particular clothing shop that sells to your potential customers? If you are not bringing the right product to the right people, there will be no money. However, if you bring the right products to the right people and for the right reasons, there will be a bond built and money will come. In the beginning, think about why you are doing what you want to do. Are you opening an after school-tutoring program to make money or to help children? If it is to make money, you will fail. If it is to help children, you will help children and you will make money. People will respond to your attitude and your "why" much faster and for longer than your "what and how".

No matter what, just keep going forward!

What About You?

So, what is stopping you? Are you afraid of failing or afraid of succeeding? Sometimes we fail because we never get started. I am supposed to be spending today writing the second chapter of my dissertation but instead, I am writing about success and failure. I am going to fail at the dissertation process if I don't start writing but I cannot make myself sit down and write it. If I start that project, I will complete it and I will succeed at my ultimate goal of getting a Ph.D. So, why can't I get started? I don't know but every day for the past two weeks my intention has been to set aside some time to write the chapter. So far, I have the title page and have it numbered and formatted correctly and that's it.

I don't have an excuse, I just haven't done it, but I know that I will. I know without a doubt that the only reason I haven't succeeded at that project is because I haven't started it. So, why haven't you started your project or started on your path to success? Sometimes starting is the hardest part. When was the last time you started an exercise program? I do it all the time… Seriously, getting dressed and out the door is the hardest part of working out for me. Once I am dressed and out the door, I always complete the workout.

So, how do you get started on a project that you are either afraid of or just don't know how to do? Sometimes, it is as simple as picking up the phone or walking into an office and asking for help from a stranger. It can also create many more difficulties for you than simply getting started on your project or your dream. What is the worst thing that can happen? You can make yourself depressed because you are not making progress. You can lose sleep and literally have anxiety attacks because it's all you think about and you're not making progress. Or it can be as simple as picking up the phone. It's your choice.

For women, things can be difficult to break through glass ceiling. I have been told many times in my career that I would have to work harder because I was a woman. There was never even any shame or embarrassment in their voice or actions when they explained it to me… none, just matter of fact "you're a woman so this is going to be harder for you". I actually had a male city councilman tell me one time that "if you were a man, there'd be no question about who the next chief would be, but you're not". Remember my opening when I said sometimes those that stood in my way helped me succeed? He, and many more just like him, helped me succeed and not because I had something to prove to them. They helped me because they showed me how much the world needed people like me to succeed to show people like him that he's not that important… to the rest of us.

There is no system in place to help us – there is no "good ole girl network" and you weren't raised to be a businesswoman or even a leader. There most certainly is a "good ole boy network" and it has created Presidents, Congressmen, CEOs, and many successful leaders. Most of the time, women face the opposite of a good ole girl network when other women seem to be working against them rather than helping them. So, how do you get started when there is no one to help you? The fact is that there are people that will help you. There are several state and federal agencies designed to assist women getting started in business. At the end of this book, I have listed all those agencies for the state of North Carolina and for anyone living outside my home state; I have listed the federal agencies and web addresses.

How do you get help if starting a business is not the dream you are searching for? If you need help losing weight, starting college or finishing high school, or learning how to design a garden to grow vegetables? You ask someone to help you. Not earth-shattering information and nothing you don't already know. Ask someone to help you and they will. If you don't know who to ask, then seek out a consultant or life coach (remember that this is what I want to do – help people like you) and they will help you. Go to the community college and someone there will help you. There are job coaches, small business experts, and other local, state, and federal agencies at the college that are there to help you. There are often free classes at the community college that cover almost any kind of questions you may have and they're most likely free of charge. Not only will these classes help you understand or learn about new things, but they will also offer you an opportunity to do something different if that means only that you are doing something for yourself for three hours a week. Do it.

Even in the darkest night, there's always a light.
Find it!

Key Takeaways and Action Items:

- Reflect on why you want to pursue your dream or goal. Ensure it's purpose-driven, as this will sustain you during challenges.
- Tackle a small, manageable part of your project to build momentum. For example, outline a plan, make a phone call, or research your next steps.
- Connect with someone who can help you. Use local resources like community colleges, small business agencies, or life coaches to gain the knowledge and tools you need.
- Acknowledge what you may need to give up—time, comfort, or other commitments—to achieve your bigger goals.
- If you're facing unique challenges, explore state and federal programs designed to support individuals like you. Find mentors or like-minded individuals to build your support network.
- Focus on progress rather than perfection. The most crucial step is to *start* and keep moving forward. Don't give up, regardless of how long it takes.

CHAPTER EIGHT

Attacking The Hill... Aka Your Fears

If you are going to conquer your fears, you first need to admit that you have a fear and be able to say it out loud. For example, if you are afraid of getting old then just say it. We all do things to keep us from aging. Anyone ever paid 50 dollars for anti-aging cream? Did it work? Of course it didn't work, it is not possible to reverse the aging process. Not with creams, not with surgery, not by exercising, and not by being afraid of it. What stops the aging process is death. That's it. Death stops the aging process, nothing else. So, don't fear getting older. Embrace it, while you keep your skin moisturized, exercise, and eat healthy. Don't fear anything for very long. Tackle it and move on. What about other fears? There is a unique beauty in aging, and we should all learn to recognize it when we see it. Some of the most beautiful women I've ever seen are over 50. They exude confidence and embrace who they are at this point in their life and that makes them beautiful... well, that and the fact that they have good hair and great genes.

   I have been afraid many times in my life and of many things. The first time I remember being afraid was when my dad convinced me to slide down a waterslide into deep water. He promised that he would catch me, so I did it and he did not catch me – he wanted me to learn how to swim. I remember thinking as a very small child, first that he tricked me and then that I needed to breathe. I fought to get to the top of that water and the first thing I saw when I got up and out of the water was my dad who was close enough to grab me if I failed or panicked. He, and my mother have always (and still are) close by to catch us if we fall – the beauty of having young parents is that they stay around a long time.

I have had that same experience many times in my life and every time there was someone close enough to catch me in case I panicked or failed. Believe me, there have been many times that I have needed someone to support my crazy ideas and to tell me to step off the cliff. There is always going to be someone to catch you if you fall or to help you refocus and build your foundation. You have to trust that you will recognize the need for help and ask for it. You also have to have someone around that you trust to tell you the truth. Truth is the most important thing in your path to success.

Have you heard the old saying that when things get tough, the tough get going? Well, as simple as that seems it is the truth. If something seems insurmountable to you, step back and take a running start at it. The harder the task, the harder you should attack it. I attended the 213th session of the FBI National Academy for law enforcement leaders in 2003. There were several physical aspects of that academy that were extremely difficult for most of the people there. I met a few running partners during the academy and one had knee problems. One day while we were on a particularly long and hard run (up and down hills and in muddy terrain) she made a statement that has stuck with me ever since. Looking up the muddy road and seeing a steep hill ahead she began to speed up (after running between 3-4 miles already). Surprised, between breaths I asked her why we were speeding up. She calmly replied that the only way to get up a steep hill is to attack it and rather than slowing down and dreading it, we sped up and attacked that hill.

The moral to that story is that nothing is hard enough to stop us from starting, doing it well, and finishing it with a positive conclusion. No hill is high enough to keep us from getting to the top. When something seems hard, get a running start and attack it like you are running for the finish line.

If you don't know where to start, then take a deep breath and call for help and keep calling until you find that one person that takes an interest in you and points you in the right direction. You will not die if someone says no, your feelings might be hurt but it won't kill you. If someone says no, say thank you and call someone else. Eventually, someone will say yes and at the end of the day when it's all said and done, each of those people (even those that said no) helped you in some way to get better at what you fear.

I have never accomplished anything in my life without help from someone else. I got my confidence and determination from my parents, my help in business from several friends, and help with my educational endeavors from both family and friends. I even have someone around who reminds me once in a while that I'm getting too big for my own britches (that sounded quite southern) and that I need to calm down a little bit (and that's an important person for me to have around). I learned how to ask for help and I learned how to take advice from friends and I learned that I couldn't fail as long as I keep trying. I am confident that I succeed at many things because of the people and experiences I've had. I am also confident that my mission in life now is to help others succeed.

If something scares you or intimidates you or makes you nervous… however you choose to say it, attack it and own that fear. By nature, we fear the unknown and once something is known to us, we no longer fear it. So, if you're shy and can't imagine yourself calling a bank and asking for money then call the bank and ask for an appointment to meet with someone next week. Then spend this week attacking the hill by doing research and preparing a business plan and preparing yourself to ask for help. Seek advice from a business specialist, take a class on how to market your business, or meet with a small business analyst to help you make these plans. Go to the appointment confident that you will succeed, and you just might walk out of there with a check. Worst-case scenario, you will walk out of there with more knowledge than you had when you went in.

As you are "attacking the hill", remember those who have tried and failed before you and learn from their experiences. Read Michael Jordan's biography and listen to him talk about not making a basketball team, then flip to the pictures and see him holding up the fifth NBA championship trophy. Read about Thomas Edison, or Apple, or Microsoft and hear stories about how many times these people (who are the richest people in the world now, and more importantly they have impacted almost every human life on the planet) had to rebuild or reboot or re-engineer something before they found the right combination.

Remember that **why** you are doing something is more important than what you are doing. Remember that if the first person you ask to help you is not interested in you or your dilemma, then keep going until you find someone that is. The only person who can cause you to fail is you… the only person that can cause you to fail is you.

The responsibility for success or failure lies with you. Accept that and stop letting someone or some thing stop you from succeeding and justifying it by blaming those things. You can succeed.

It doesn't matter what you want to do, whether it is painting a wall, losing weight, starting a workout regiment, changing jobs, or starting a business. Know why you want to do it, then what you're going to do and finally, how you're going to get it done. Don't be upset when someone suggests a different way to do something but never lose your passion about doing it because it is your passion. Most of my ideas need adjusting, just as this book will have editors, critics, and helpful friends that all offer suggestions for change. I will probably make some of those changes – because they will make this better and more likely to help you. I want to be successful so I will listen to those who can help me be better at what I am doing. I have never written a book before (I'm sure you've probably guessed that by now) so I need lots of help to get this done. Even with my ego and my level of self-confidence, I will ask for help and listen to those that are kind enough to offer it.

Finally, as you attack the hill remember what your priorities are and never lose sight of your family obligations and what matters most to you. Don't give up on your dreams and know the difference between a dream and a fantasy. Enjoy the fantasy but don't chase it. Chase the dream until you catch it and then take time to enjoy it. Remember the inspirational quote from my friend, "you can either sleep with your dream or wake up and chase it"? Wake up and chase your dream. It is extremely important to me that I do not put a timeline on my dreams. I am by most accounts too old to be chasing this dream, but it is my dream and only I can decide when I will give up on chasing my dreams. For me, the aging process is not the only thing death will stop. I will be chasing a dream as long as I'm breathing and that excites and challenges me.

If you found something in this book that inspired you or motivated you to take a positive action, then please share it with someone else. Remember that women need to help other women rather than tear them down through resentment and jealousy. There is enough success to go around, and everyone wants different things so embrace your dreams and capture your success. When you succeed, help someone else and always keep your family first because in the end they are all that matters.

Peace comes to those that look out the window..
and then step outside!

Key Takeaways and Action Items:

- Write down a fear you've been avoiding and brainstorm actionable steps to overcome it.
- Evaluate the people you keep close. Ensure they are honest, supportive, and aligned with your goals.
- When a challenge emerges, commit to facing it head-on instead of delaying action.
- Create a network of mentors, advisors, or colleagues who can provide guidance and truth when needed.
- If faced with rejection, regroup and look for alternative pathways. Keep asking until you achieve clarity or assistance.

- Draw inspiration from successful individuals who've overcome setbacks. Read biographies or case studies of those you admire.
- Make a list of your dreams. Identify which are worth chasing and develop a loose plan to pursue them with passion.
- Stay grounded—allocate time for family and your personal priorities even as you strive for professional success.
- Encourage and support others in their journeys. Share lessons and successes while fostering collaboration.
- Move towards your goals with confidence, balancing persistence and flexibility. Remember, it's your dream—pursue it unapologetically.

Final Thoughts

I have partners in this adventure with similar goals but very different stories. Each of them are successful, accomplished women that have struggled to succeed and done so while raising children and/or helping others do so. I am proud to be part of such a strong group of women and hope that as we all chase our dream of helping others, that you are one of those people. We have established the "why" of our journey into this business and are figuring out the how. If this book helps you in any way, then you become part of the "who" and the time is now. So, we have the who, what, when, where, why, and how of our business. What about you?

Don't wait for someone else to tell you how or why to do what you have always dreamed of doing. If you want to be a tennis player, buy a $15 dollar racket and go play in the recreation league. The person you're playing might not be Martina Navratilova or Chris Everett (yes, I am that old) but pretend that you're playing in the final match at Wimbledon and play to win. If you want to be a writer, then pick up a pen and piece of paper and write (again, yes, I am that old). You may be the next Stephen King or that guy from New Bern, NC that writes all those mushy romance novels, but you won't know unless you try.

I have friends in their second or third careers who are making an impact on lots of things and people, and as I write, one of them is out of the country doing amazing things. These women work, play, donate, volunteer, and dedicate themselves to living life to the fullest every day and they inspire me to do the same. Whether they are helping someone learn to read a book or helping someone adopt a furry friend for life, these women live a life that inspires others. We should all live our lives until the very last day of it with helping others in mind. If we do this, we will close our eyes satisfied knowing that something we did that day mattered.

You can do this. It can be done. And finally, no one deserves this more than you. If you need help (and we all do) then ask for it and keep asking until someone says yes. Don't give up because it gets hard – attack the hill. Make what you do matter by helping others and creating a positive change. TODAY! Start today, not tomorrow or next week. TODAY! Good luck and remember that if I can ever help you – I always will.

Wrenn Johnson
Enjoy your life!

About Wrenn

 Wrenn Johnson is a Performance Expert and Coach and a Founding Member of Transformational Pathways, LLC. With a deep commitment to personal growth and development, Wrenn is also a member of Christian Simpson's Conscious Coaching Academy and received her first coaching certification under the mentorship of John Maxwell. Born and raised in High Point, North Carolina,

Wrenn later embraced coastal living after attending the University of North Carolina in Wilmington. She settled in Morehead City, NC, where she carved an impressive career in law enforcement, eventually retiring as the Chief of Police—a role she holds in great pride.

Beyond her professional accolades, Wrenn treasures her role as a mother and grandmother. She has one son, a wonderful daughter-in-law, and three cherished grandchildren, whom she adores. She often says, "Of all the titles I've held, being a parent is the most important, and grandparent is the best promotion I've ever received." Family is central to Wrenn's life, a value reflected in her work.

She is passionately driven by a desire to help women discover their purpose and achieve success in what matters most to them. Through her coaching, Wrenn inspires others to believe in their potential, empowering lives with purpose and fulfilment.

Work with Wrenn

Success isn't just for organisations – it's for individuals like you, striving to overcome obstacles and achieve your personal best, whatever that may be.

Wrenn works with individuals looking to transform their lives, whether it's considering a career change, building self-confidence, or simply seeking greater fulfilment. Wrenn's personalized strategies will help you take control of your path, so start today to break free from self-doubt, redefine your goals, and step into the life you've always envisioned.

With proven techniques and relatable guidance, Wrenn will help you reach your potential and achieve success on your own terms.

Don't wait for the right moment to come along – take the first step today and contact Wrenn on wrennjohnson@gmail.com, and begin your transformation. Your dream life is closer than you think!

Please Review

Dear reader,

Thank you for taking the time to read this book. I would really appreciate if you could spread the word about it and if you purchased it online, if you would leave a review.

Thank you

Wrenn

www.ingramcontent.com/pod-product-compliance
Lightning Source LLC
Chambersburg PA
CBHW041310110526
44590CB00028B/4309